101 Things To Do During A Dull Sermon

101 Things To Do During A Dull Sermon

by **TIM SIMS**

Illustrated by **Dan Pegoda**

With a Little Help from:
Rickly Christian
Will Eisenhower
Tom Finley
David Lynn
Jim Pegoda
Doug Peterson
Robert Price
and
Mike Yaconelli

A Wittenburg Door Book

Edited by the Keepers of the Door

Book Designed by
Gary Bell
and
Jerry Jamison

Youth Specialties, Inc.
1224 Greenfield Drive
El Cajon, California 92021
(619) 440-2333

TABLE OF CONTENTS

FORWARD

Church is great.
. . . most of the time.
And, no matter what anyone says, sermons are ok too.
. . . most of the time.
Periodically, however, something goes wrong.
Your minister has a bad day,
and the sermon ends up . . . well . . . a little dull.

It's no one's fault.
Really.
Maybe your minister didn't have time to study enough this week.
Maybe your minister had an argument with his/her spouse.
It doesn't matter, because, whatever the reason, the result is the same: a dull sermon.

The question is: "What can you do about it?"
Well. You could ask the minister to resign. But that takes a lot of time and energy and, unless dull sermons happen all the time, the problem may not be your minister. After all, your minister is a human being subject to the same lapses that happen to all of us.

So, now we are back to the question, "What can you do about it?"

That's a good question and this book has a lot of good answers. 101 of them, actually. Each and every one of them will keep you, your family and the people sitting next to you in church occupied for many a dull sermon to come.

In fact, we have the feeling that after you use this book for awhile, you will be looking forward to the next dull sermon. There are six different categories of things to do (Higher Learning, Diversions, Musings And Meditations, Church-Er-Cise, Fine Arts and Facts and Figures). Most of the ideas in this book can be shared with those sitting around you, so they can "enjoy" the sermon, too.

Not only can the suggestions in this book keep you and yours occupied during the dull times, but you might even show the book to your minister. That might be just the motivation your minister needs to keep those dull sermons from ever happening again.

1

HIGHER LEARNING

Stimulating Your Mind When The Sermon Doesn't

1 Jots and Tittles

Locate all of the typing ~~misteaks~~ mistakes in the church bulletin.

2 Word Power

It pays to increase your word power. Whenever you hear a word you are unfamiliar with during the sermon, write it down and guess at a definition (that's how some theologians arrive at *their* definitions.) Check your guesses with a dictionary, Bible Dictionary, theological encyclopedia or ask your neighbor.

3 A Modest Proposal

Write a letter to the church board proposing a lottery to help finance the new building program. Be certain you have done adequate research by playing the lottery a few times yourself before making your proposal. (Deduct your losses by describing your activity as religious research.)

4 Bird Brain

See how many state birds you can list. Match the state birds you have listed with church members who look like one of the birds.

5 Six Days Shalt Thou Labor

Since many people in your congregation only work five days a week, devise a list of jobs for the sixth day and submit it to those people after church. Job ideas might include work on the church property, publicity, visitation, painting your swimming pool, etc. Your fellow worshippers will be *so* glad for your help in this matter.

6 Hymn Memorization

Take advantage of this lull in your interest to learn those troublesome second and third verses of hymns—you know, the words you mumble while trying to keep up with the tempo. A Bible dictionary may help you make some sense of the lyrics.

7 Methuselah

See how many words you can make out of the word Methuselah.

Score:

1-9 words	Some boring spots in sermon
10-20 words	Lots of boring spots in sermon
21-40 words	Totally boring sermon
41 or more words	Even the minister is bored and has decided to help you.

8 Song of Solomon

Using the Old Testament book, The Song of Solomon, as your guide, compose an oozing love letter to a prominent church member. Leave it inside a hymnal (unsigned, of course). Your gushy literary effort will keep you awake this week . . . and perk up someone else next Sunday.

9 Go Tell It On The Mountain

Write a note to your preacher offering to loan him all of your camping gear if he will take off for a few weeks.

10 Multiple Choice Church Quiz

See if you can answer the tough question below. On the back of the pew in front of you there is probably a shelf for hymnals, attendance cards and pencils. In the churches of many denominations you will find a piece of wood attached to each side of the shelf with two ¾" holes drilled through like this:

What are these holes for?
Check the correct
answer below:

A. Place to hook fingers so person can have help in standing up.
B. Slot for rolled up church bulletins.
C. The termites are ferocious here.
D. Glass eyeball holder.
E. Special clamping device for tubular aluminum frame to prop up the old man in front of you.
F. Holder for communion glasses.
G. All of the above.

Answer: All of the above.

11 Ananias and Sapphira List

With due consideration for the net worth of each member and their motives for giving, list the names of the "Ten Most Likely To Be Struck Dead During The Offering".

12 In My Arm
His Handiwork I See

With the freckles on your arm, make up some new constellations and name them. Advanced suggestion: See if you can find someone with freckles on *their* arm close enough for you to make up new constellations and name them. (Note: you can use your face, if you have a mirror, or you can focus your mirror on someone *else's* face.)

2

GAMES

Staying Awake
Through Play

13 Alpha Through Omega

Listen for your preacher to use a word beginning with "A", then "B", and so on through the alphabet. You may get stuck on "Q" unless your preacher is a fundamentalist preaching against homosexuality.

14 Millenial Bingo

When you hear any of the words or phrases in the squares below during the pastor's sermon, mark the square with an "X". When you have five in a row (across, up and down, or diagonally) stand up and shout, "It's the rapture!"

Last days	1335 days	Credit Cards	Ezekial	144,000
Kissinger	trumpet	Another church building	antichrist	Daniel
tribulation	nuclear bomb	FREE	Hal Lindsay	Babylon
666	caught-up	Bank Collapse	Israel Tour	McDonalds
Revelation	return	armageddon	Beast	1000 years

15 A-Millenial Bingo

Wait for someone playing Millenial Bingo to stand up and shout, "It's the rapture!" Then stand up and shout, "No it's not!"

21

16 Cast Lots

All you need are knee pads, some dice, your offering money and . . . well, maybe this isn't such a good idea.

17 Who Is The Anti-Christ?

See if you can find the identity of the antichrist hidden in the letters below. It may be spelled horizontally, vertically, diagonally, forward or backward.

```
L H I B M G T U M I X Y
D S A Q O C B P O R F E
W E I H T B U R O P W E
I L B L H A R E V B D U
P I L D E B R O S X M A
Z T O R R B X B L M I I
S A U T I W V B L M I W
P X H G N K K L S W W J
A Z A G L I L G B U U L
R O W B A U C T G H K F
U D J F W P Y K R E V M
```

18 Rebus

Create a rebus using the sermon text for the day.
Example: "Lighten my eyes, lest I sleep the sleep of
death." Ps. 13:3

 +

 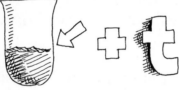   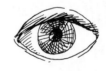

   THE

OF

23

19 Hands Up

If you are part of a lively congregation where there is a lot of hand raising, try cataloguing the various styles of raising hands as you observe them during the sermon.

People who use this "two-arm toss" position probably have been moved by one of the sermon points . . . either that or they are listening to the Super Bowl on a transistor radio and someone just scored a touchdown.

This is a popular position, although it doesn't show quite the same level of uninhibited spontaneity as the two-arm toss. Also, if the arm is raised at an angle and the palm of his or her hand is facing down, you better check whether the worshipper is wearing a Nazi uniform.

This means the air conditioning is on too high.

"You have a run in your nylon. Can't you dress better for church?"

This means, "illegal headcovering: There is a woman in church wearing the most ridiculous hat I've ever seen."

This quickly conveys the message, "Honey, it's your turn to yell at the kids."

"No pumpkin, I think it's your turn to discipline the brats."

"I have to go to the bathroom . . . real bad."

20 Jumbled Context

Open your Bible at random and point to a verse. Write it down. Repeat the process until you've received a personal message from Scripture. Example: ''Pay their expenses so that they may shave their heads . . . (Acts 21:24) . . . and your Father who sees in secret will reward you.'' (Mat. 6:18)

21 Marble Roll

Sit in the back pew and roll a handful of marbles under the pews ahead of you. After the service, credit yourself with ten points for each marble that made it to the altar.

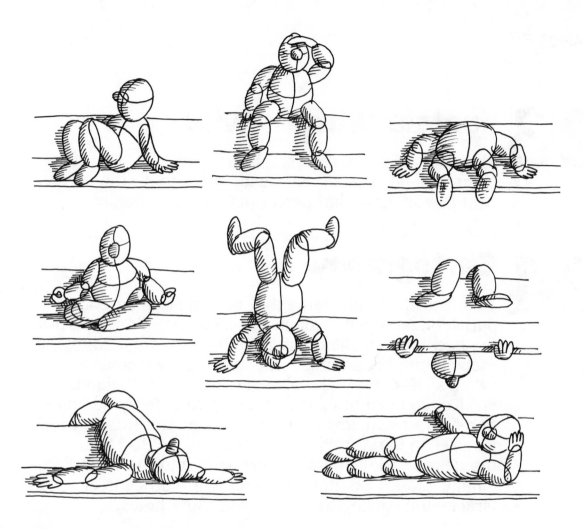

22 Pew Warming

By experimentation, try to determine how many comfortable pew sitting positions you can discover.
You will kill a lot of time before you realize there are NO comfortable pew sitting positions.

23 Footsie With A Twist

Play footsie with the person in front of you. If he/she turns around, shake your head and point to the person next to you. Give that person a disgusted look.

24 Cartography

This is a traditional game that has entertained bored parishioners down through the centuries. Simply turn to the back of your Bible and pass the time by reading the maps there. Try adding some funny place names to "Paul's Missionary Travels" like Siberia and Tijuana, Mexico. You can bring the maps up to date by adding anti-aircraft gun emplacements in Iran and Russian SAM missiles in Syria. With your pencil, move PLO troops into the Bekaa Valley and send terrorists into the West Bank. Finally, launch US and Soviet nuclear warheads at Israel—thus giving the Holy Land more holes.

25 Squirt Gun

Tuck a squirt gun up your sleeve. See how many people you can squirt before they find out it is you. For best results, sit in the front row balcony and shoot down.

26 Flashcards

Make a set of score flash cards like the ones Olympic judges use to score sporting events. Judge this week's sermon on these categories:

1. Quality of monotone
2. Use of obscure vocabulary
3. Lack of interesting illustrations
4. Number of irrelevant points

27 How Observant Are You?

Look all around you for exactly ten seconds. Now, close your eyes and then answer these questions:

A. How many people are sitting in the pew with you?
B. What row are you sitting in?
C. What is the preacher wearing?
D. What is the color of the walls?
E. What is the title of this book?
F. How can you read these questions with your eyes closed?

3

DIVERSIONS

A Collection Of Slightly Disruptive Activities

28 Pinch (First Variation)

Modestly, discreetly, with the utmost in decorum, pinch yourself to stay awake.

29 Pinch (Second Variation)

Modestly, discreetly, with the utmost in decorum, pinch your neighbor. This should keep both of you awake.

30 Pencil Service Project

Sharpen the golf pencils in the racks on the backs of the pews. A pen knife will help you accomplish this vital, but often overlooked, task in the life of the church.

31 Missionary Pilot

Using bulletins or attendance cards for raw materials, design, test and modify a collection of paper airplanes.

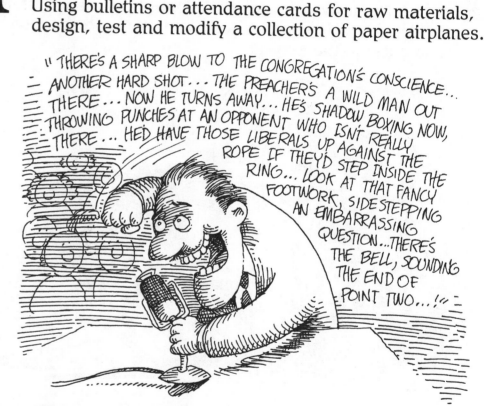

" THERE'S A SHARP BLOW TO THE CONGREGATION'S CONSCIENCE... ANOTHER HARD SHOT... THE PREACHER'S A WILD MAN OUT THERE... NOW HE TURNS AWAY... HE'S SHADOW BOXING NOW, THROWING PUNCHES AT AN OPPONENT WHO ISN'T REALLY THERE... HE'D HAVE THOSE LIBERALS UP AGAINST THE ROPE IF THEY'D STEP INSIDE THE RING... LOOK AT THAT FANCY FOOTWORK, SIDE STEPPING AN EMBARRASSING QUESTION...THERE'S THE BELL, SOUNDING THE END OF POINT TWO...!"

32 Play-by-Play

If you are seated near the rear of the auditorium, away from people, quietly "broadcast" the sermon (or the entire service) using the jargon of a sports announcer.

33 Growl

Listen for growling stomachs. Count how many different kinds of growls you can hear. Time them to see which one goes on the longest.

STEVE, YOU CAN EXHALE NOW. CHURCH HAS BEEN OVER FOR FIVE MINUTES. STEVE?

34 Breath Control

Time yourself holding your breath. You may wish to keep records from week to week to note your improvement.

35 Request

Pass a note to the organist asking whether he/she plays requests.

36 Choral Distraction

Any number of techniques can be used to create laughter behind the preacher's back, but care must be taken lest you are discovered and reprimanded from the pulpit. This is a definite improvement on an old diversion: Watching the choir members trying to stay awake.

37 Anonymous Letter

Requires scissors and glue. Cut out individual letters from bulletins, hymnals, or whatever's available and arrange them into an anonymous note (remember the ransom notes in the old movies?). In the letter (to be sent to the preacher) suggest guest speakers or candidates to replace him in the pulpit.

38 Yawn

See if a yawn really is contagious.

39 Cue Cards, First Variation

Help the preacher by giving him a responsive audience.
From the front pew hold up large cards that will help the
listeners respond in unison (in the tradition of silent
movies and melodramas). Sample cards: "Amen", "I
hear you", "That's right", "Ha-ha-ha", "Ooooh", etc.

40 Cue Cards, Second Variation

Similar to the previous diversion, only these cards are designed to help the preacher keep in touch with the moods of the audience. Sample cards: ''Get to the point'', ''Tell another joke'', ''You're fading fast'', ''We're praying for you'', etc.

41 Pew Crawl

Start from the back of the church and try to crawl all the way to the front, under the pews, without being noticed.

42 Back Row

Join the young people on the back pew. Ask to borrow one of their Walkman's.

43 Potty Break

Raise your hand and ask permission to go to the bathroom.

44 Turn The Other Cheek

Slap your neighbor. See if he or she turns the other cheek. If he or she doesn't, raise your hand and tell the pastor.

45 Contemplative Snoozing

Learn to sleep while kneeling. If someone wakes you up, simply say "Amen" and they will be embarrassed that they disturbed you.

46 Prayer Request Cards

Using the Prayer Request Cards located in the rack of the pew in front of you, compose some rather juicy little pieces concerning torrid love affairs, absurd habits or some shocking confession. Don't sign a name . . . or, on second thought, sign someone else's name.

47 To Bernie Or Not To Bernie

Pass a note to someone named Bernie, but first make sure there is no one named Bernie in your congregation. (Note: if you are attending a synagogue, try the name Ricardo.)

48 Misplaced Amen

Shout a loud "Amen!" at the conclusion of a sentence that isn't particularly inspiring. Watch to see whether anyone else chimes in with an "Amen!" or whether the sermon suddenly becomes livelier in response to your response.

49 Last Of The Red Hot Sermons

As a creative way to earn money during a dull sermon, walk amidst the congregation with a load of hot dogs and shout, "Hot dogs! Get your hot dogs here!" To help create a "baseball atmosphere," the organist may even agree to occasionally play "Charge!"

50 Wristwatch Alarm

Once the pastor begins his sermon, set the alarm of your watch to beep after twenty minutes . . . and every five minutes thereafter until he is finished.

51 Applause

Though you are groggy, loudly applaude the pastor at the conclusion of his sermon. He'll think he made a vivid impact on your life. As an exercise of Christian charity, keep the *real* reason to yourself.

52 Liberal Church Altar Call

If you are attending a liberal church, come forward to be "born-again" toward the end of the sermon: that will really throw things into a tizzy.

53 Nasal Hymns

Whip out a handkerchief and blow your nose. Vary the pressure exerted on your nostrils and trumpet a rendition of your favorite church hymn.

46

54 Offering Plate

Bring along an offering plate and start passing it around during the sermon. Then quietly change your seat so the offering plate comes back to you full.

55 Contact Lens

Blink and squint dramatically, then get down on your hands and knees. If the person next to you should ask, tell him you've just lost your contacts. Crawl quickly toward the door.

56 Creative Endings

If the sermon is droning overly long, take things into your own hands for a quick finish:

A. Pretend to pass out; slump unconscious onto the aisle floor.

B. Begin sneezing uncontrollably. (This may, however, result in an attempted exorcism.)

57 Smelly Socks

Refrain from washing your socks for eleven days. During the sermon, remove your shoes.

58 Lawrence Welk Bubble Counter

If sermon goes over fifteen minutes, start blowing bubbles.

59 Baptismal Surprise

Hide in the Baptismal Fount wearing a "Creature From The Black Lagoon" outfit. Stay out of sight, but begin calling softly, "Pastor Billy Clyde . . . Oh, Pastor Billy Clyde . . .". When the preacher finally stops his sermon and comes over to see who is calling his name, grab his tie and see if you can pull him in.

60 Alarm

Unravel a thread from the back of a hymnal. Tie one end to the pew in front of you, the other end to your wrist. As the congregation leaves, someone will break or trip over the thread, thus alerting you in time to exit with the crowd.

61 Amazing Gaze

Stare intently at the preacher. Count how many times the preacher looks into your eyes. See if you can make him sweat. See if you can hypnotize him into imitating a chicken.

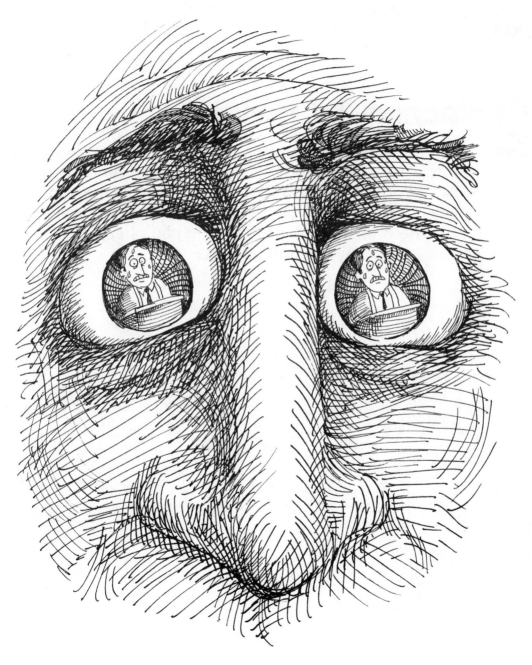

62 Hearing-Aid Humming

Sit in the hearing-aid section of the sanctuary. During the sermon, whisper to several old folks that the preacher wants everyone to hum. Begin humming ''Amazing Grace'' and encorage all the hard-of-hearing saints of the Lord who are sitting near you (and can't hear the message anyway) to hum along.

63 Sticky Hymnal

Glue the pages of hymnals together.

64 Quick And Easy

A. Tug on the nearest necktie to see if it's a clip-on.
B. By unobtrusively drawing your arms up your sleeves, turn your shirt or blouse inside out.
C. Try to raise one eyebrow.
D. Crack your knuckles.

Diverrionr

E. Find the oldest church bulletin and Bible study ditto sheet in your Bible. This will tell you how long it's been since you last really read your Bible.

F. If you have a retractable ball point pen, take it apart and shoot the ink cartridge straight up in the air with the spring.

G. Fix an empty gum wrapper so it looks like there is still gum it it. Fool the person next to you.

H. Pretend to be four years old.

I. Figure out how many angels can dance on the end of a pin.

J. Figure out how many angels can dance on the end of your nose.

K. See how many categories of noses you can find: fat noses, pointy noses, flat noses, etc.

L. Try to signal the minister that his zipper is down.

M. Come to church with your bathing suit under your dress clothes. During the sermon remove your outer layer of clothes so that only your bathing suit is on so you are ready to go to the beach as soon as the sermon is over.

N. Try to guess what the ushers are doing in the narthex.

O. Join the ushers in the narthex.

P. Think about your chin(s) for an entire minute.

Q. Twiddle your thumbs.

R. Twiddle your neighbor's thumbs.

S. Get everyone in your row to twiddle their thumbs.

T. Keep shaking your head "no" as if violently disagreeing with everything the minister is saying. See how long it takes to get him distracted.

U. Wiggle your ears enough so that the people behind you will notice.

V. Wiggle the ears of the person in front of you.

W. Duck as they swing at you.

X. Drop a hymnal and count how many turn around to see where the sound came from.

Y. Try to think of another "quick and easy" thing to do so we'll have a full alphabet worth—from a to z.

Z. Write it in here:_____

4

Musings And Meditations

Creative Use Of
The Imagination

65 Imagined Interruption

What if someone stood up in the middle of the sermon and asked a question or made a comment? Or just stood up? How many of the old ladies would faint in embarrassment? Certainly the entire congregation would be wide awake. Picture this scene in your mind. If you do it long enough, you may find yourself gaining the courage to try it.

66 Comforting Comparison

List some things that would be even *more* boring than listening to this dull sermon, for example:
A. Making out this year's Christmas list.
B. Balancing your checkbook.
C. Cleaning your comb.
D. Reciting the pledge of allegiance forwards and backwards.
E. Humming a Steve Miller song.

67 Zaccheus

Devise ways of climbing into the balcony without using the stairs.

68 Ballgame Worry

If your favorite team is playing in the east, worry about how much of the game you're missing.*

*For West Coast churchgoers only

69 Creative Responsive Readings

Come up with some new responsive readings for your congregation. An example might be:
PASTOR: Hello Dolly, well Hello Dolly.
CONGREGATION:It's so nice to have you back where you belong.
PASTOR: You're looking swell, Dolly.
CONGREGATION: We can tell, Dolly.
PASTOR: You're still growing, you're still showing, you're still going strong.
CONGREGATION: And also with you.

70 Saganize

Carefully listen to each word the preacher says, but imagine how it would sound if Carl Sagan was speaking. Try not to burst out laughing.

71 Remember

Try to remember what last week's sermon was about. Try to remember what this week's sermon is about. Try to remember the last time the preacher didn't mention money.

72 𝕴𝕟𝕜 𝕭𝕝𝕠𝕥 𝕿𝕖𝕤𝕥

Make ink blots on the bulletin and have a companion
guess what they represent. Now analyze your
companion's responses and suggest that your companion
see a psychiatrist.

73 Psalming

When the preacher makes a dramatic or melodramatic statement, complete it with a rhyming phrase. The more ridiculous, the better. Example: Pastor: "We count people because people count," then you add, "and our rivals are impressed with our amount". *Or,* Pastor: "God helps those who help themselves," then you add, "and our chocolate chip cookies are baked by elves". *Or,* Pastor: "To join this church you've gotta believe," then you add, "and put in ten bucks when the offering's received."

74 Getting The Picture

Keep your mind in touch with the sermon by outlining it with illustrations. Use simple cartoons, even stick figures, to capture the ideas.

JOSEPH *and* MARY'S FLIGHT TO EGYPT

5

FINE ARTS
Handling Boredom
With Class

75 *What Child Is This?*

On the Sunday before, "accidentally take home a hymnal. Hollow out the pages like they do in spy movies and fit in a miniature tape recorder. Make a tape of a baby crying. Then go to church with the modified hymnal and wait for the right moment. Once the sermon has begun, discreetly begin the tape. Make sure the crying doesn't begin right away (maybe five minutes into the cassette) so it will seem to have started on its own. Also be sure the volume is up enough to be heard through the book cover. With the hymnal in its rack and you sitting back and away in the pew, no one will be able to figure out whose child is causing all that ruckus.

76 *Nail Sculpture*

Clip your nails. Use the clippings to make little "fish" symbols on the back of the pew in front of you.

77 *Glowing Sermon*

Have you ever noticed that if you leave your eyes wide open as long as possible without blinking, you will see the walls change colors and the preacher outlined in flourescent white? Shapes will shift and change, hues will flash and sparkle.

It's fun, try it . . . but don't go overboard.
We don't want your eyes to turn into dried-out raisins.

78 Keep An Eye Peeled

Use felt pens from the Sunday morning Bible study supply closet to color phony eyeballs on your eyelids. People will think you're wide awake through the whole sermon.

79 Loud, Have Mercy

Build a remote control for the church sound system and when you start to get tired of the sermon, very gradually turn the volume up until the sermon stops . . . or everyone has evacuated the building.

80 Rehash Mash

There are no new episodes of the famous TV series "M.A.S.H." Your assignment is to direct a new season's worth of new shows, but first, due to contractual complications, you must recast the characters. Imagine that the people in your church are auditioning for the parts. Choose from the congregation the individuals most suitable for the roles of Hawkeye, B.J., Colonel Potter, Hot Lips, etc.

PUT JACKET SLEEVES IN JACKET POCKETS.

81 Fake Head Trick

During the week, take some time to sculpt and paint an exact likeness of your head. While in church wear the fake head on top of your shoulders. Your real head will be hunched down inside of your jacket and you will be free to sleep or, if you bring a flashlight, you can read the Sunday paper. If you are a particularly clever artist, you may want to try the Fake Head And Body Trick which would leave you available for beach parties or nice Sunday morning drives.

82 *Mind Control*

Practice your powers of ESP on the person sitting in front of you. Start with simple tasks, such as trying to get them to scratch their head by thinking over and over again, "Scratch your head. Scratch your head. Scratch your head." Once you've developed a knack, move on to more complex commands like, "Throw your hymnal. Throw your hymnal. Throw your hymnal." or "Take your shoes off your feet and put them on your hands. Take your shoes off your feet and put them on your hands. Take your shoes off your feet and put them on your hands."

CHURCH-ER-CISE

Aerobics For
The Church Pew

83 *Finger Twirl*

Move your left index finger in a circle clockwise three times. After some practice, try moving the same finger in the opposite direction.

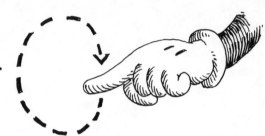

84 *Lip Lick*

Lick your lips.

85 *Foot Feat*

Step on your left foot with your right foot while trying to raise your left foot off the ground.

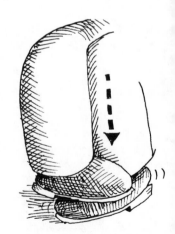

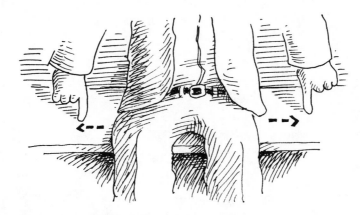

86 *Rear-ender*

Indicate with your two index fingers two points on the pew five inches away from your body to the left and right of you. Then race your buttocks back and forth between the two points.

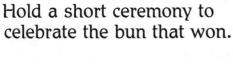

87 *Closing Ceremonies*

Hold a short ceremony to celebrate the bun that won.

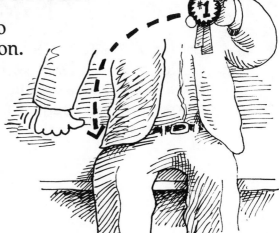

88 *Weight Lifting*

Even dull pastors love firm believers, so make good use of the hour. Gather two hymnals in each hand and practice arm thrusts and curls. Great for the biceps. Hook your toes beneath the pew in front of you and perform leg lifts.

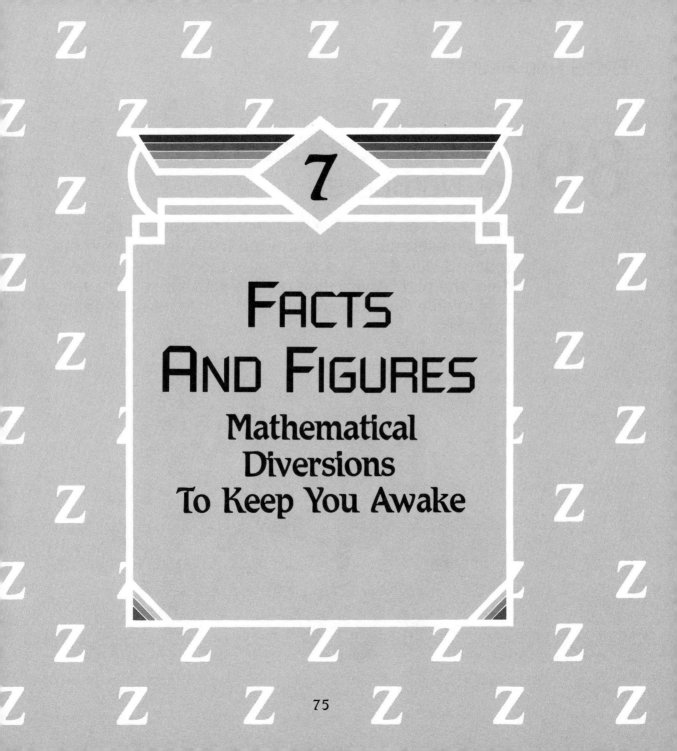

7

FACTS AND FIGURES
Mathematical Diversions To Keep You Awake

89 The Hairs On Your Head Are Numbered

Yes, but do you know the number? Try counting them during the sermon. If there are too many to count on one Sunday, divide it up and count only those hairs on one side of the part. A variation on this activity, suitable for upper middle class congregations, is to count the number of toupees.

90 1000 Years

If, in the Lord's sight, a day is as a thousand years and a thousand years is as a day, how many years would this sermon be consuming if it were a thousand year day? Share your answer with the pastor.

91 Counting

A. Count new haircuts.
B. Count people who need new haircuts.
C. Count babies you like.
D. Count babies you don't like.
E. Count your ribs.

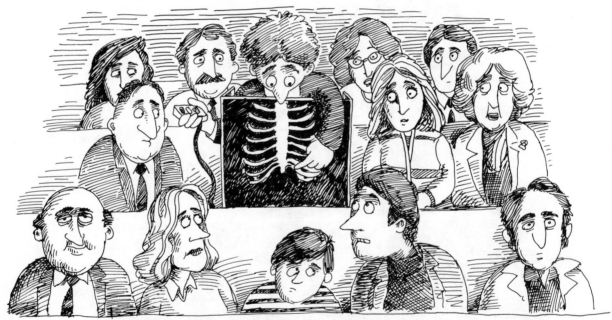

F. Count your neighbor's ribs.
G. Count your black eyes after counting your neighbor's ribs.

H. Count bald heads.
I. Count your teeth with your tongue.
J. Count how many elderly ladies have purple hair.
K. Count how many dead animals the church women are wearing.
L. Count how many women look like dead animals.
M. Count everyone in the balcony. Calculate how many people it would take in the balcony to collapse the floor.
N. Count how many people in the choir should never be allowed to sing . . . anywhere.
O. Count how many things you wish you were doing right now.
P. Count how much money you would pay the minister to stop preaching.
Q. Count the pieces of gum underneath your pew.
R. Count the little kids underneath your pew.
S. Count the entire congregation.
T. Count the number of people in the congregation who are not listening to the sermon either. Maybe it would be faster to count the number of people still listening to the sermon.
U. Count how many runs down the slopes you could have skiied by now.
V. Count how many times you have thought about getting rid of your minister.
W. Count the organ pipes.
X. Count the songs in the hymnal that you don't understand.
Y. Count the number of times your minister has said "in closing" in today's sermon.
Z. Count people counting.

92 Blessed Be The Tie That Clips

If you attend one of the few remaining churches where the men still wear ties, you can while away some time by keeping tabs on how many are wearing a "clip-on" tie. For variety, you can try to count the number of women (or men, nowadays) who are wearing "clip-on" earrings. (Extra points if you caught the "tab" pun in the first sentence.)

93 Faster Than A Speeding Sermon

Sound travels at seven hundred sixty-four miles per hour at temperatures of thirty-two degrees Fahrenheit, even during rush hour. Estimate how long it would take the pastor's sermon to reach other cities. Estimate how long it would take the sermon to run down to the corner drug store, pick up a candy bar and bring it back to you. Also, you may be interested to know that sound travels faster at higher temperatures. Therefore, you might ask the church janitor to turn off the air conditioning so the sermon would reach you sooner and end earlier.

94 Weeping And Wailing

Often, when one baby in an otherwise silent congregation begins crying loudly, other babies will join. By getting the baby nearest you to start crying (take away his pacifier, make ugly faces, etc.), see how many other babies you can get to cry all at one time. Count the babies crying and compare with the number that a friend can make cry during the next lull. Highest number wins. Score bonus points if you can make the preacher cry.

95 Choir Scales

Guess the weight of each member of the choir. This may be difficult since most choir robes look like Sears pup tents. Place bets and compare results with the person next to you. Then, query each choir member after the service to determine who had the closest guess.

96 Calling Dr. Luke

Count the number of people who cough or clear their throats. An interesting study is to calculate a coughs-per-minute ratio and compare it to the coughs-per-minute ratio during the prayer time or the announcements.

97 Creative Visitor Embarrassment

List ways to embarrass visitors. It will be difficult to think of things that churches haven't already done, but try. (Here are some suggestions to get the creative juices going: Have the visitor list all the books of the Bible by memory; Ask the visitor why he/she hasn't been coming to church.)

98 Ego Tally

Keep weekly figures on the number of times the preacher says "I," uses a personal illustration, or gives a personal opinion.

99 Clothes Call

Look around and see how many mistakes in attire you can find. For example, are there any inside-out socks, shirts or gloves? How about collars that need turning down, zippers unzipped, buttons misbuttoned, nylons running or shoes untied? Oh, by the way, be careful not to look *too* hard at a couple of these.

100 Preacher's Salary

Estimate the preacher's salary and figure the amount he/she is making for each minute of the sermon.

101 101 Things Sequel

Think of 101 *other* things to do during a dull sermon.